Who Was
Sam Walton?

by James Buckley Jr.

illustrated by Ted Hammond

Penguin Workshop

To Stephanie and Jason—TH

PENGUIN WORKSHOP
An Imprint of Penguin Random House LLC, New York

Visit us online at www.penguinrandomhouse.com.

Library of Congress Cataloging-in-Publication Data is available upon request.

ISBN 9781524792701 (paperback)   10 9 8 7 6 5 4 3 2 1
ISBN 9781524792718 (library binding)   10 9 8 7 6 5 4 3 2 1

Contents

Who Was Sam Walton?

Sam Walton loved to sell. Although he was only in second grade in 1925, he went door-to-door selling magazines to his neighbors in his Missouri town. He knocked on doors up and down his block, carrying a sample of the magazines he sold. Neighbors were amazed to see this little boy standing up straight and speaking clearly and proudly. He sold one magazine for a nickel. He sold another for a dime. Pretty soon, he figured out he should try to sell more of the ten-cent magazines than the five-cent ones!

It was not just magazines. Sam raised bunnies in his backyard and sold them as pets. He and his mother milked a cow in their backyard. They bottled the milk and cream . . . and Sam sold it.

As Sam grew up, he kept selling. He had a newspaper route and was always adding new customers. He worked in a small store that sold a little bit of everything. He worked in restaurants, providing food and drinks to hungry visitors. Sam also took odd jobs, helping people around their yards or making deliveries.

Sam's family was not poor, but they were not rich, either. They certainly could use all the extra money that Sam could bring in. For Sam, selling was a way to help his family. It just turned out that it was something he was really good at.

It also turned out that what Sam probably sold best was himself. From the time he was a little kid, he was confident and friendly. He loved meeting new people, and he was never afraid to shake someone's hand and say hello. He became a very popular person at school because he made sure to greet everyone he met with a big smile. Sam's boyhood friend Everett Orr later said that Sam had something magical about him. "He made friends easily. People sort of flickered toward him, even when he was young."

By the time Sam finished school, he knew he wanted to keep selling . . . and to keep meeting people. He opened the first store of his own in Arkansas in 1945. By the time he was in his late thirties, Sam Walton owned stores in many small towns in the Midwest. He made sure to visit them all, and he was always ready to shake a customer's hand. There were no strangers at Sam Walton's stores.

When Sam was forty-four, he started an even bigger version of his store, a new way to sell even more things to more people.

He called his new store Wal-Mart.

CHAPTER 1
Farm Life

Samuel Moore Walton was born on March 29, 1918, in Kingfisher, Oklahoma. His family owned a small farm there. Sam's father, Thomas, had lived on farms his whole life.

Sam later wrote that his father had been a great trader. Thomas loved making deals with people. Thomas once traded his watch for a pig to feed his family. He even traded other farms to get the one they lived on in Kingfisher!

Before Sam's mother, Nancy Lawrence, married Thomas and joined him on the farm, she had gone to college for a year. Attending college was very unusual for women at this time. As her family grew, Nancy made sure that they knew how important education was.

Even though Sam was little, he helped on the farm. The family kept chickens, and Sam often gathered their eggs with his mother. The farm had pigs, too. Sam would feed them by pouring table scraps into their pen.

In 1921, Sam's brother, James, was born. From the time James was a baby, everyone called him "Bud." Sam and Bud did everything together.

Together, the boys played on the farm and helped with any chores they could. Thomas sometimes helped his two young sons ride together on the family's horse, Trix.

Farming was a hard business, however. A lot of farmers struggled to earn enough money to stay on their land and keep farming. World War I had ended the year Sam was born. In the years afterward, sales of wheat, corn, and other farm crops slowed down.

During the war, American farmers and businesses had been successful, selling food and supplies to the US Army. After the war, those sales dropped dramatically. Many businesses and farms were forced to close. Thomas was having a tough time selling the crops he grew.

Thomas Walton had a big decision to make. Though he loved life on the farm, he had to make sure his family was taken care of. He was no longer making enough money from his farm.

Thomas had an uncle who ran a company that helped people buy farms. He decided to sell the family farm and take a job with his uncle's company. Sam and Bud helped pack the car and the family drove to a new home in Springfield, Missouri. A year later, the family moved again, this time to the town of Marshall, Missouri.

World War I (1914–18)

In 1914, a terrible war broke out in Europe. It was so large and involved so many countries that it became known as the Great War. On one side were Germany and several smaller countries. On the other were France, the United Kingdom, Russia, and Serbia. The two sides fought because the assassination of Austrian archduke Franz Ferdinand had sparked a conflict among the nations.

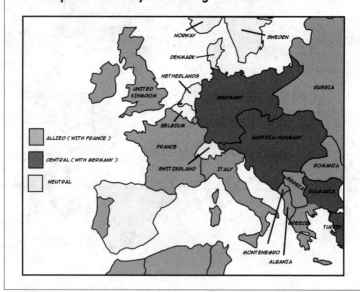

The two sides fought for nearly five years. Millions of soldiers, sailors, and civilians died as a result.

In 1917, the United States entered the war on the side of the United Kingdom and France. And Japan and Italy joined the German side. American soldiers were sent to the battlefields of Europe to help to defeat Germany and its allies.

On November 11, 1918, Germany signed a peace agreement, ending the war.

Living in town was very different than living on a farm. Young Sam still wanted to help his family, though. On the farm, he had helped sell eggs and milk. Living away from the farm, he learned to earn money in other ways.

In town, there were many more people living closer together. Sam thought that maybe there was a way to earn some money with all the new customers he now had as neighbors.

CHAPTER 2
Salesman and Scout

Sam was only in second grade, but he wanted to get right to work. He got an after-school job selling magazines. He walked from door to door in Marshall. He learned to speak clearly to adults, to be polite, and to convince them to buy from him. One magazine he sold, called *Liberty*, cost five cents. Another called *Woman's Home Companion* was ten cents. Sam learned quickly to try to sell more *Woman's Home Companions*!

In 1929, the Great Depression began in America. Millions of people were suddenly out of work. Many could not afford to keep their homes and farms.

Sam sometimes went with Thomas to visit the people who had borrowed money to pay for their farmland. Some of the families could not pay back the loans. Watching his father work made a big impression on Sam. He saw families struggling to pay their bills during and after the Depression. Sam saw how hard it was for families to earn money. And to complicate matters, many farmers in and around Missouri faced a natural disaster that was ruining their land: an extreme drought.

Because of the Depression and the drought, the US economy was very weak. People struggled to earn even a little money. Sam worked as many jobs as he could to help his parents. He and his mother again started a business selling milk from a cow they had bought and kept in their backyard. Sam did the milking, Nancy separated the cream and milk and bottled it.

The Great Depression

On October 29, 1929, the stock market—where people bought and sold shares of stock (small portions of large companies)—crashed. That is, its value went way, way down very quickly—almost overnight. Shares of stock were worth much, much less than what people had paid for them. Some were worth nothing at all, and people lost all their money.

Suddenly, people and businesses could not pay back what they had borrowed earlier in the prosperous decade known as the Roaring Twenties. The banks that loaned that money had to close. Businesses closed, too. The people who worked for those businesses lost their jobs, and many lost their homes. Millions of people were out of work and had to wait in line at soup kitchens just to eat.

For the next several years, the effects of this crash and the massive loss of money had a huge effect on America. This time became known as the Great Depression.

After the US government created programs to give people jobs and to help reopen banks, the Great Depression finally began to fade by the late 1930s.

They sold the bottles to friends and neighbors. The family's farm life was paying off—not many people in Marshall knew how to milk a cow!

Sam also raised baby animals such as rabbits. And once the bunnies were old enough, he sold them to other families.

The Dust Bowl

During the 1930s (sometimes called the "Dirty Thirties"), a terrible drought hit the Southern Plains region. A drought is a long period without rain.

Without rainwater, the soil on farms and fields in the center of the country dried to dust, and much of this dusty soil blew away in the strong wind. The entire area became known as the Dust Bowl. Without moist, fertile soil, farmers could not plant

crops and had nothing to sell. People, farm animals, and crops were killed by dust storms. The drought's effects ruined many family farms.

Kansas, Oklahoma, Texas, and New Mexico were the states hit hardest by the Dust Bowl. Missouri and Arkansas were also affected. Millions of people had to leave the region and move to other parts of the country. For many, their lives as farmers were over.

The severe drought did not end until 1939.

Sam also started delivering newspapers. He had so many paper routes that he had to ask other boys to help him; he made money on the papers those boys delivered, too!

Even though Sam was working hard and going to school, he made time to join the Boy Scouts. He and other Scouts met every week to learn and practice new skills like tying knots, woodworking, and first aid. Sam was determined to be the best Scout.

The top rank was called Eagle Scout. To earn this rank, a Scout had to gain twenty-one merit badges for learning new skills or doing projects. Sam told all his friends that he was going to be the youngest Eagle Scout in Missouri!

Wanting to be number one was nothing new for Sam. Nancy encouraged her boys to always reach for the top. In fact, Sam later wrote, "She told me I should always try to be the best I could at whatever I took on."

The Boy Scouts

Robert Baden-Powell, a British military officer, founded the Boy Scouts in 1908 in England. He had written a book about how he had trained his soldiers, and he thought that young boys might

like to learn some of the same outdoor skills.

Baden-Powell organized boys aged eleven to fifteen into small troops or patrols. They worked together to learn about nature and wildlife, camping, tying knots, and other crafts.

The Boy Scouts grew quickly, and by 1910, troops were being formed in the United States.

In the Scouts, boys earn awards called merit badges for learning new skills. A Scout who follows the rules and earns twenty-one badges can qualify for the highest rank, Eagle Scout.

Today, the organization is called Scouts BSA. In 2019, girls were allowed to join Scouts BSA. There are more than 2.4 million Scouts in more than two hundred countries around the world.

The family moved again when Sam was thirteen. This time, their home was in Shelbina, Missouri. Sam's best friend in their new town was Everett Orr. Everett saw right away how friendly Sam was. He could tell that people liked Sam and liked to be around him.

Sam and Everett were both Boy Scouts. When Sam was thirteen, he earned his twenty-first Scout merit badge. He had done it—he was the youngest Eagle Scout in the state!

Sam's final merit badge to become an Eagle Scout had been for lifesaving. One afternoon he got a chance to put his training into action. Sam, Everett, and some other kids were playing in a nearby river. A boy named Donald was swept downriver by the strong current.

Sam dove in and swam toward his friend.

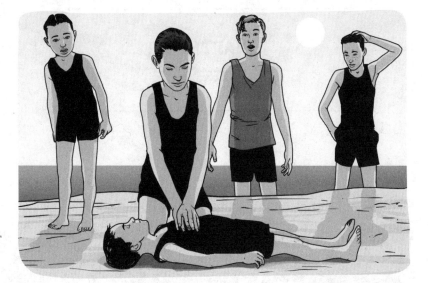

He had learned both swimming and lifesaving in the Scouts. Sam pulled Donald back to the riverbank. Everett and the other boys stared in amazement as Sam blew air into Donald's mouth and pushed on his chest to revive him. It worked! Donald started breathing again— Sam had saved his life!

Sammy Walton Rescued a Boy from Drowning!

Scouting Taught Former Marshall Boy What to Do.

CHAPTER 3
Sports Star

Just before Sam started high school, he and his family moved again, this time to Columbia, Missouri. Columbia was the biggest town the family had lived in yet. One reason they chose it was because it was home to the University of Missouri.

Nancy wanted her sons to make college part of their plans, and she thought living in a college town was a good idea.

Sam's high-school plans included playing sports. Back in Shelbina, he had played on a neighborhood football team with friends. His father was one of the coaches. The young team took on other towns' youth teams.

At Hickman High in Columbia, Sam quickly showed that he knew what he was doing on the football field! By tenth grade, he was the team's quarterback. Sam played for three seasons and he loved to say that he never played in a losing

football game at Hickman. (The team did lose some games . . . they were just games that Sam didn't play in!) With Sam as the team's leader, Hickman won the Missouri state championship twice. Sam later wrote that playing on the football team convinced him even more that he wanted to be the best at everything he did—in sports or in business.

In high school, Sam did much more than just play football. He still delivered newspapers after school, and he also found time to join many different clubs on campus. He joined the Speech Club, in which students learned to give talks in public and to communicate well with other people. Sam joined the Latin Club, the Library Club, and even the Magic Club.

Sam was very popular among his classmates. They elected him the student body president. "Sam had a great smile on his face and felt like everybody was his friend and the world was something he could conquer," remembered classmate Clay Cooper.

When Sam was a senior, Hickman's basketball coach asked the school's football star to join the team. Bud was already playing basketball, and Sam jumped right in and played guard. This team won a state title, too!

Sam also made his mother very proud by earning a spot on the honor roll for his grades.

Most Versatile Boy - SAM WALTON

When Sam graduated high school in 1936, he was named "Most Versatile Boy" by his classmates. *Versatile* means that you can do many different things well. That was certainly Sam!

CHAPTER 4
Big Man on Campus

Just as his mother had hoped, Sam attended the University of Missouri. And just as he had been at Hickman, Sam was very active at his new school. He joined a fraternity called Beta Theta  Pi. (Fraternities and sororities are organizations formed by students who live and spend time together.) Sam soon got the job of "rushing," or encouraging other young men to join the fraternity. He drove around the state to meet students who were coming to the university. Sam met them with a smile even before they got to Columbia!

Sam was soon a big part of the university's campus life. He put to good use the lessons he had learned selling magazines and being in his high-school speech club. "I learned early on that one of the secrets to campus leadership was the simplest thing of all: speak to people coming down the sidewalk before they speak to you." All those students that Sam met elected him University of Missouri student body president.

To help pay for his classes and books, Sam was *still* delivering newspapers! He also worked in restaurants, and he put his Scout training to use as a lifeguard at town swimming pools. He even worked briefly in a local variety store, which sold hundreds of different products from clothing and toys to soap and tools.

In college, Sam also joined a group called the Reserve Officers' Training Corps (ROTC) that helped train future army officers. He spent the summer of 1939 at an army camp in Kansas, training with ROTC. Later, he was chosen as the president of an ROTC honor society at Missouri.

As his time in college neared its end, Sam knew he had to make a decision. He really wanted to go to a business school, such as the famous Wharton School in Pennsylvania. But he knew that his family could not afford it, and that he had to find a full-time job.

ROTC

Many parts of the US military include officers who learned their skills while still in college. Some went to military colleges, while others took part in classes and training at private or public universities.

Officers have been trained by American colleges since the early 1800s. However, in 1916, during World War I, an official national organization was formed for such training. Reserve Officers' Training  Corps (ROTC) groups were set up at colleges around the country. Today, young men and women who take part in ROTC can earn college credit and scholarships while also learning to be military officers. The US Army, Air Force, and Navy each have their own ROTC programs. When ROTC students graduate college, they can become officers in a branch of the US military.

Sam had studied business and economics in college. And of course, he had been a salesman since he was very young.

In 1940, Sam met with two retail chains—large companies that owned many stores.

J.C. Penney was based in New York and had stores in big cities throughout the Midwest. Sears, Roebuck and Co. was an older, bigger, and more famous company in Chicago. Its mail-order business also made it one of the country's largest businesses.

Both J.C. Penney and Sears offered Sam a job. He chose to work for J.C. Penney. He was twenty-two years old and was proud to begin his first job in a store.

CHAPTER 5
Getting to Work

Sam started work at a J.C. Penney store in Des Moines, Iowa. He was in a program that trained young men to become store managers. The leader of the program, Duncan Majors, became a mentor—a trusted adviser—to Sam.

Mr. Majors made sure the young men worked very long hours, often from six thirty in the morning to seven at night, six days a week. Even on Sundays, the trainees met at Mr. Majors's house. After they learned what a big paycheck their boss got as a bonus from J.C. Penney, the young men were inspired to work even harder.

Sam loved learning about his new job. At lunch, he would sometimes visit other big stores in the area to see how they did things differently than at J.C. Penney. When he wasn't checking out the competition, he took only short lunch breaks so he could spend more time in his own store.

One time Sam met J.C. Penney's founder and owner, James Cash Penney. Penney was an American business legend. His company was founded in 1902 with a single store in Wyoming, and he went on to build a huge national chain

James Cash Penney

of J.C. Penney stores. Sam remembered watching Mr. Penney tie a package using the least amount of string possible. This taught Sam that saving any money you could was good for business, even if it was just the cost of an extra bit of string.

Sam also learned a lesson from Mr. Penney that he would try to follow in all of his stores: Treat people right, help them save money, and they'll come back. Penney's stores did not try to sell each item for the highest price they could. They tried to sell a bigger variety and more items. People seemed to buy more if they thought they were saving money on each sale.

While Sam was working in Iowa, World War II started in Europe and Asia.

World War II

In 1939, Germany attacked several countries in Western Europe in an effort to expand its territory. Italy soon joined the Germans, and over the next six years, the war expanded to many parts of the world. In Asia, Japan—an ally of Germany—invaded China, the Philippines, and other nations.

In Europe, Great Britain, France, Russia, and many other smaller countries fought back against the German and Italian attacks. In 1941,

after Japan attacked the Hawaiian Islands at the Pearl Harbor naval base, the United States joined the war in Europe and Asia, too.

In what came to be called World War II, the two sides battled on the sea, on the land, and in the air. Millions of soldiers and sailors died. Millions of civilians were also killed by German forces whose mission was to destroy all Jews and other people they didn't like. The war finally ended in 1945 with the defeat of Germany and Japan.

In 1940, a new law called for young men to be chosen for the armed forces, or "drafted." When America entered the war in 1941, Sam knew that he could soon be drafted. While he waited for that call, Sam left his job with J.C. Penney. He found a job in Claremore, Oklahoma. He was twenty-three years old.

One evening after work, he met a young woman named Helen Robson at a bowling alley.

Helen was also a college graduate and knew some people that Sam knew at the University of Missouri. Helen was working for her father's company in Claremore. Sam liked Helen and her bright spirit right away. They started dating and soon planned to be married.

But the US Army had other plans for Sam. In 1942, he was drafted. Because of his time in ROTC, he became an officer called a lieutenant. However, when the army doctors examined him, they found that he had a small problem with his heart. It was not serious, but the army said he could not serve in combat—he would not be going into battle. Instead, he was given an army job that kept him in the United States.

Sam left Helen behind in Oklahoma while he began his work in California, but he returned in 1943 to marry Helen in Claremore. For the next two years, the newlyweds moved from army base to army base as Sam's assignments changed.

Sam's main job was with army security. He worked at bases to make sure they were safe from attack and that soldiers behaved properly. And his second army job was protecting the factories where airplanes and other war machines were made.

In 1944, the couple had their first child, Samuel Robson Walton, whom they called Rob.

In 1945, World War II ended, and Sam left the army. He and Helen began to plan their life together. During the war, they had moved many times because of Sam's job with the army.

Now Helen wanted to settle in one place. She wanted to live in a small town.

Sam knew that he could use what he had learned in school and at J.C. Penney to run his own business. The couple found a store for sale in Newport, Arkansas. Sam borrowed some money from Helen's father, Leland Robson, and added all of his own savings. Sam Walton's first day in charge of his own store was September 1, 1945.

CHAPTER 6
Sam the Storekeeper

Sam's new store was actually part of a larger group of stores. The Ben Franklin Company worked with managers like Sam to open stores in small towns. The company gave the managers training and business plans and supplies. In return, the managers had to buy all the items they would sell from Ben Franklin.

Sam's Ben Franklin store sold a little bit of everything. People could buy clothing—but nothing too fancy—dishes, kitchen appliances, candy, sewing supplies, toys, stationery, hand tools, and some home decorations. He sold all sorts of personal items, too, from toothpaste to shampoo to makeup. These kinds of stores were known as variety stores, or "five-and-dimes."

Just as he had when he sold magazines, Sam always looked for a way to sell more. He figured out that he could buy his goods for less money than The Ben Franklin Company was charging him. He discovered that if he bought something for just a little bit cheaper somewhere else, and sold it for a little less, he could sell *more* of it.

For example, if Sam bought a pack of socks for fifty cents and sold them for seventy-five cents, he made twenty-five cents in profit. What if he could buy the same socks somewhere else for forty cents, and then sell them for sixty cents?

He earned only twenty cents profit per pair, but counted on selling a lot more socks for sixty cents than for seventy-five cents. Selling more products for less money was a business system Sam used for the rest of his life.

Sam also came up with fun ways to get people to come into the store. He sold popcorn from a machine on the sidewalk in front of the store. People could follow the smell of hot popcorn right to the store's entrance. Serving soft ice cream was another way to bring people in.

Five-and-Dimes

Stores that sell many different kinds of items are called variety stores. They have been around since 1879 when Frank Woolworth opened a store in Utica, New York. Originally, Mr. Woolworth didn't sell anything in the store that cost more than five cents. But later, he added some more expensive items that cost ten cents, and the stores became known as "five-and-tens" and sometimes as "five-and-dimes."

Woolworth soon added many more stores and the company became the largest chain of five-and-dimes in the United States. It was certainly not the only one. Most small towns had such stores, some that were part of chains and some that were just in a single location.

Five-and-dimes gave people a place to buy many small things they needed for their homes, from clothing and hardware to toys for the kids and gifts for their families. They could buy cooking supplies, sports gear, candles, lightbulbs, and much, much more.

As time went on, prices eventually rose beyond nickels and dimes. But the variety store became a huge part of the American shopping experience.

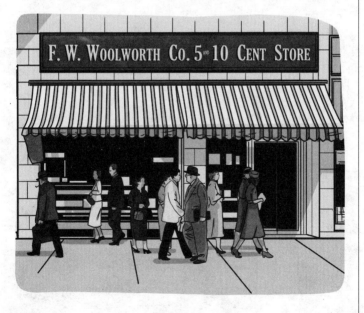

Sam spent nearly all his time working, but he did find time to help his children in Boy Scouts and on sports teams. He joined organizations like the chamber of commerce—a local business network. Naturally, he was elected president of the chamber. He also taught Sunday school at the Presbyterian church and helped raise money for the local hospital.

Sam had learned to hunt quail from Helen's father. Together, Sam and Mr. Robson often went to the woods on weekends with their bird dogs. If they were lucky, they brought home quail for supper. Bird hunting became Sam's favorite pastime. He later took up tennis and, as he had on the football field, he worked hard to become very good at the sport. He was just as competitive as ever.

As Sam's Ben Franklin store grew busier and busier, Sam's family grew bigger. John Walton was born in 1946. James was born in 1948, and daughter Alice in 1949. Still, Sam spent most of his time working, leaving Helen to raise their four kids. He did have help from his brother, Bud, who had joined him in running the store after leaving the army himself in late 1945.

While living in Newport, Sam decided that he wanted to open stores in other cities, and he often drove to look at possible locations. He also made trips to buy new products to sell in his Newport store. Driving on the winding country roads in Arkansas took up a lot of time, though, and Sam did not like to waste time. So he started hiring small airplanes to fly him around.

After almost five years, Sam had turned his little store into a shining success. His Ben Franklin was the most successful in the state. Unfortunately, the man who owned the building that Sam rented saw how well Sam was doing. The property owner wanted his son to take over Sam's Ben Franklin store, so he refused to rent to Sam once their agreement was up. Sam was crushed. There was nothing he could do. "It was the low point of my business life," Sam later wrote. Sam felt like he had to start all over again.

CHAPTER 7
Life in Bentonville

After Sam left Newport in 1950, he felt that he had to pick himself up "and get on with it, do it all over again, only even better this time." He found a space for his next store in Bentonville, Arkansas. There were already three other stores nearby, but a little competition never bothered Sam.

Though this new place was still part of the

Ben Franklin chain, Sam called it Walton's 5&10. He made sure to get a ninety-nine-year rental agreement on the building so that he wouldn't have any more surprises from his landlord.

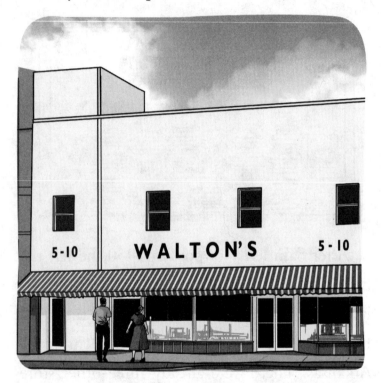

In the early 1950s, variety stores looked very different than they do today. Instead of rows of open shelves full of goods, the store's products were all behind cases built under the counters. Several clerks and cash registers were stationed around the store. Clerks removed each item as customers asked to see it. People couldn't just pick things off the shelves by themselves. Pretty soon, however, Sam helped change that. He heard of a store in Minnesota that was trying "self-service."

After a long bus ride there and back to check it out, he made his Bentonville store self-service, too!

Sam's first airplane

That bus ride and his past experiences flying from Newport led Sam to buy his first airplane in 1954. Sam quickly learned to pilot it himself. His brother, Bud, was not too thrilled with this plan. He had been a pilot during World War II. "Sam knew nothing about airplanes," Bud remembered later. "I couldn't believe he was going to buy one.

I was real concerned." A few years later, Sam bought an even bigger plane. Flying around to his stores, usually by himself, became part of his weekly routine.

Flying made it easier to do what he really wanted—open more variety stores. Throughout the 1950s, Sam opened store after store, all in small towns in Arkansas and nearby states.

While Sam was very busy, often working sixteen hours a day (he would sometimes arrive at his office at 4:30 a.m.!), Helen was busy with the four Walton children. She ran a Girl Scout troop, worked for her church, and made sure her kids always got healthy meals. They were an active family. Helen later joked that it seemed like one of them was always in a cast after an accident. When Sam took time off, the family made long car trips to places like Yellowstone National Park or the Grand Canyon, or to visit Helen's family in Oklahoma.

The Walton children didn't just have fun,
though. All of them eventually worked at
Walton's 5&10. They stocked shelves, helped

customers, sold popcorn, and learned the rules of business from their dad. The shop's main rule was "the customer is always right."

The Walton children also took after their dad by delivering copies of the *Arkansas Gazette* newspaper.

Life was going well for Sam and his family, but he was already looking ahead to the next new challenge.

CHAPTER 8
The First Wal-Mart

By the early 1960s, Sam focused on a new idea. He thought he could make prices even lower by building bigger stores. That would let him sell more products to more people. He could charge lower

prices and still earn a profit. He went to the Ben Franklin business managers with his idea, but they weren't interested. Sam decided it was time to go out on his own.

About eight miles from Bentonville, he found a place for his new, larger store in Rogers, Arkansas. He borrowed money from family and friends and from a local bank. A friend, Bob Bogle, helped him come up with the store's name—Wal-Mart.

On July 2, 1962, the first Wal-Mart opened

Wal-Mart Grand Opening, 1962

in Rogers. Sam made sure that prices were low and that there were lots of different products to choose from. The goods covered huge tables. Sam soon added new racks of shelves. It was a hit from the start. Crowds lined up outside to await the opening of that first Wal-Mart.

One Wal-Mart was not enough. Soon Sam was opening several Wal-Marts a year. But things didn't always go smoothly. In front of a new Wal-Mart in Harrison, Arkansas, Sam stacked giant piles of watermelons for sale. In the parking lot, the store was also offering free donkey rides

to young children. The opening day was extremely hot and the watermelons started exploding! The donkeys walked through all the watermelon mess and added some of their own. Customers had to walk through the smelly slime to get into the store!

Bud and Sam in a Wal-Mart store

Exploding watermelons aside, sales at the first Wal-Mart stores went up year after year. Sam made plans to open even more Wal-Marts. Bud partnered with him to open some of them. And other family members gave or loaned money to help the chain of stores grow. By the end of the 1960s, Sam had opened thirty-eight stores.

Even as Wal-Mart grew as a company, Sam continued to be involved in everything. He visited each store several times a year. He carefully looked at what was selling and what was not. He made sure that his store managers put the customer first and made shopping a fun experience. He even wore a Wal-Mart name badge when he visited; it read simply "SAM."

Sam insisted on calling people who worked at Wal-Mart his "associates." They were not just employees, he said, he wanted them to be part of a team. "I never in my life heard him tell one of the associates that they weren't doing a good job," said Grace McCutcheon, who worked at Wal-Mart No. 2. The associates called him "Mr. Sam." Sam's role as a sort of cheerleader for his associates would continue for the rest of his working life.

Sam and Wal-Mart were not alone in opening new stores. In the early and mid-1960s, several large companies were starting chains of variety stores. They offered many different products, most at very low, or discount, prices. Stores with names  like Kmart, Target, Woolco, and Kresge were popping up all over the United States.

 For Sam, those other stores became just teams to beat on the field. Most

of those stores were in large and medium-size cities. Sam continued to focus on places like Bentonville and Rogers. "There was much, much more business out there in small-town America than anybody, including me, had ever dreamed of," he wrote.

In 1970, Wal-Mart sold stock in the company for the first time. That meant the company raised money by selling part of the business to the public. The Walton family still owned nearly all of the Wal-Mart stock. But selling some of it let Sam raise money that he could use to open even more stores. By 1977, Sam had opened 190 Wal-Marts! By 1982, he had more than five hundred!

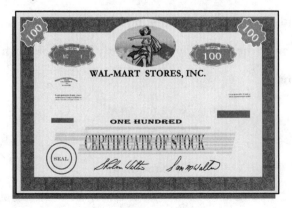

The Wal-Mart Cheer

When he visited a Wal-Mart, Sam Walton always tried to encourage his associates. He was famous for climbing up on a chair or a table and leading everyone in the Wal-Mart Cheer. Sam said he got the idea after visiting factories in Korea where group cheers were common.

"Give me a W!

Give me an A!

Give me an L!

Give me a squiggly!"

(Sam meant the little symbol that divided *Wal* and *Mart* in the company logo for many years. Sam showed how to "give a squiggly" by shaking his hips.)

"Give me an M!

Give me an A!

Give me an R!

Give me a T!

What's that spell?

Wal-Mart!

Who's number one?

The customer . . . always!"

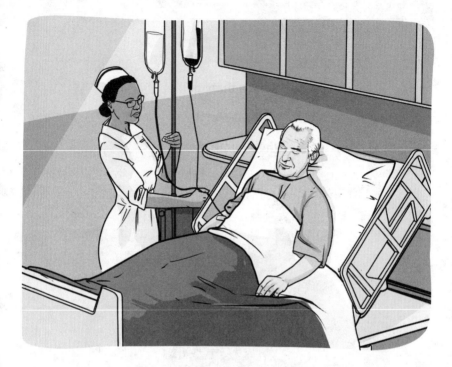

Things seemed to be going very well, but in 1982, Sam got some bad news. Doctors told Sam that he had cancer. Like any other challenge in his life, Sam faced it head-on. He got the best doctors and found the latest treatment. Sam was given a new medicine that had recently been discovered. He started taking it, and in about a year, his cancer was not making him sick anymore.

The people of Bentonville were thrilled by the company's success and Sam's recovery. Many of them worked for Sam and also owned some stock in Wal-Mart. On October 8, 1983, the town held a "Sam and Helen Walton Appreciation Day." The events were to thank the Walton family for all they had done to transform the little Arkansas town. There was a parade, a picnic, and a concert with country music stars, and the junior high school was renamed in Sam's honor.

People from around the country called or wrote to congratulate Sam. President Ronald Reagan called Sam and Helen. His call was broadcast over the speakers. He told everyone at the party, "I want to pay a special tribute to [Sam and Helen] for being an outstanding example of dedication,

President Ronald Reagan

hard work . . . and the spirit that has made this nation great and strong."

Sam enjoyed the party but got right back to work. To encourage his associates and managers, Sam often gave them challenges. Early in 1983, he challenged all of Wal-Mart to reach a growth of 8 percent in profits by the end of the year.

Profit is the money stores make after they pay all their bills. Sam promised that if they came through, he would dance a hula on Wall Street in New York City. Well, Wal-Mart topped that 8 percent mark. On March 15, 1984, Sam put on a grass skirt and a flower crown, and did a hula dance in front of TV cameras on Wall Street!

All those profits helped Wal-Mart keep growing. By 1987, the company had more than one thousand stores. It was an important and exciting year for the Waltons.

CHAPTER 9
Richest Man in America

In 1985, everything changed for Sam and the Walton family. *Forbes* magazine published its annual list of the richest Americans. Sam had been on the list in the past. But this year, to many people's surprise, Sam was number one! All the stock that he owned in Wal-Mart—the many small parts of the entire business—was then worth more than $2.8 billion. That was more than the personal wealth of any other single American.

All of a sudden, people all over the world wanted to know everything they could about the Waltons, and especially about Sam. But he had little interest in telling them. He wanted to take care of his family and his stores and his associates, and for the business to keep getting bigger and better. He didn't think anyone needed to know how he and his family lived their lives.

The curiosity only grew. Reporters visited Bentonville to see how Sam lived. They watched him get a haircut at the local barbershop.

They took pictures of him in his beat-up old pickup truck with his bird dog, Roy. They told readers that Sam often shared a hotel room when he traveled for business, rather than spending the money on a room just for himself. Instead of having a pilot fly him around in a fancy jet, Sam flew his own small plane. Very few wealthy people acted the way Sam did!

Even as he became world famous, Sam focused on growing Wal-Mart. He had made it a goal to become the biggest and best store chain in the country. Little by little, Wal-Mart grew

1965

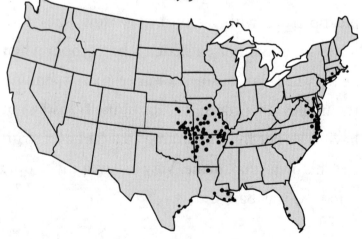

1973

bigger than other chains, with more stores and higher sales. By 1989, the company included more than 1,500 stores.

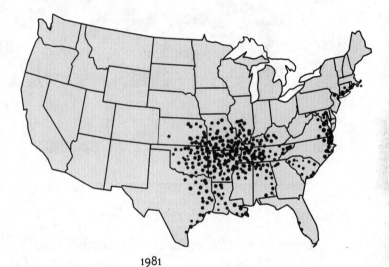

1981

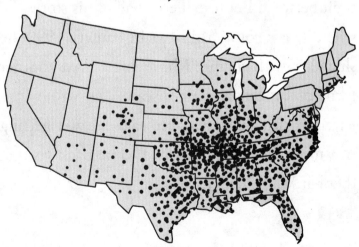

1989

Sam also still wrote to his associates each month in the company newsletter. And he spoke to them over the satellite TV connection he had built between Bentonville and all of his stores. So when he got some bad news in January 1990, he shared it with them. "I have contracted another form of cancer, a bone disease," he wrote in a letter to the associates. He said he was getting treatment and that he hoped to be back visiting them at Wal-Marts very soon.

By 1990, Sam had done it. He had beaten all the other stores. Wal-Mart became number one, surpassing Kmart to become the largest store chain in the United States. Wal-Mart had more stores and earned more profits than any other chain. The company went on to open its first store in Mexico in 1991. Sam, of course,

Wal-Mart's first store in Mexico, 1990s

was not satisfied. He continued to challenge his associates to help Wal-Mart grow even bigger!

By 1991, however, Sam's cancer had gotten worse, and he had to slow down. He could not visit with his associates, but he enjoyed spending time with his family. He and Helen had ten grandchildren by then. Sam and Helen also focused more on using their great wealth to help others. For years, the family had helped build schools and hospitals, and had helped students by establishing scholarships. They also gave money to libraries, museums, and to their church.

On March 17, 1992, Sam and Helen welcomed a special visitor to Bentonville. Sam was too ill to travel, so President George H. W. Bush went to Arkansas. He was there to award Sam the Presidential Medal of Freedom for his contributions to business and to charity. "It was the greatest day of my life," Sam wrote afterward.

Presidential Medal of Freedom

The Presidential Medal of Freedom is the highest award given to American civilians—those who are not part of the military.

The award was established by President Harry Truman in 1945. Since then, presidents have given the honor to nearly six hundred people. Recipients are chosen based on their

President Harry Truman

contributions to the nation in fields such as entertainment, sports, charity, science, culture, and business.

The award ceremony is usually held at the White House.

Just three weeks later, Sam Walton died from his ongoing illness. He was seventy-four years old. At the time of his death, he and his family were worth $23 billion. There were 1,735 Wal-Marts in forty-two states, plus two in Mexico.

The Walton family (Helen passed away in 2007) continues to own the majority of Wal-Mart stock. As of late 2018, the children and grandchildren of Sam and Helen together were worth more than $163 billion, by far the richest family in America. Rob, Jim, and Alice were each in the top fifteen of the *Forbes* 400, as well. Rob became chairman of Wal-Mart. Jim works for the company. Alice runs part of the family foundation and an investment company. (John had mostly stayed out of the family business; he passed away in 2005.)

Rob Walton

Jim Walton

Alice Walton

In the years since Sam's death, Wal-Mart has continued to expand, just as Sam had hoped it would. By the end of 2018, Wal-Mart had opened more than eleven thousand stores of different sizes. They are located in all fifty states and twenty-seven countries. The stores in the United States employ more than 1.5 million associates (and another 700,000 around the world). That makes Wal-Mart the single largest employer in the country.

All those stores come from the vision of one man: Sam Walton. He created a shopping empire by sticking to a simple plan: Sell things that people need at the lowest prices possible . . . and treat every customer right. Just as he once loved to pilot his small airplanes, in his business Sam Walton steered the Wal-Mart company in for a perfect landing.

Timeline of Sam Walton's Life

1918	Sam Walton is born in Oklahoma
1933	Moves with family to Columbia, Missouri
1940	Graduates from the University of Missouri with a degree in economics
	Begins working for J.C. Penney
1943	Marries Helen Robson
1944	Son Rob is born
1945	Purchases first Ben Franklin store in Newport, Arkansas
1946	Son John is born
1948	Son Jim is born
1949	Daughter Alice is born
1950	Starts Walton's 5&10 in Bentonville, Arkansas
1962	Opens first Wal-Mart in Rogers, Arkansas
1970	First sells stock in Wal-Mart to the public
1985	Named "richest man in America" by *Forbes* magazine
1987	Wal-Mart has over 1,100 stores
1992	Receives Presidential Medal of Freedom from President George H. W. Bush
	Dies of cancer at the age of seventy-four
2008	Mr. Sam's company changes its name to read simply "Walmart"

Timeline of the World

1918 — World War I ends

1927 — Charles Lindbergh is the first person to fly solo across the Atlantic Ocean

1929 — The Great Depression begins

1939 — World War II begins in Europe

1945 — The United States drops two atomic bombs on the Japanese cities of Hiroshima and Nagasaki, ending World War II

1953 — Scientists announce they have solved the mystery of DNA, the organic chemical that is the building block of all life

1961 — Soviet cosmonaut Yuri Gagarin becomes the first human being to reach space

1963 — The March on Washington calls for civil rights in America

1967 — Football's first Super Bowl is played in Los Angeles, California

1971 — The first e-mail is sent between two computers at the Massachusetts Institute of Technology

1976 — The United States celebrates the bicentennial, its two hundredth birthday

1989 — Demolition of the Berlin Wall begins in Germany, uniting a city divided between the democratic West and the Communist East

1993 — Mosaic becomes the first web browser program

Bibliography

*Books for young readers

Alef, Daniel. *Sam Walton Changed the World of Advertising.*
Santa Barbara, CA: Titans of Fortune Publishing, 2007.

*Blumenthal, Karen. *Mr. Sam: How Sam Walton Built Wal-Mart
and Became America's Richest Man.* New York: Viking, 2011.

Hayes, Thomas C. "Sam Walton Is Dead at 74; the Founder of Wal-
Mart Stores." *The New York Times*, April 16, 1992.

Trimble, Vance H. *Sam Walton: The Inside Story of America's
Richest Man.* New York: Dutton, 1990.

Walton, Sam. *Made in America: My Story.* With John Huey. New
York: Doubleday, 1992.